Lakes & Mountains of New Zealand

Published by Colour Library Books for
GORDON & GOTCH LTD

Text by Joe Ryan.
First published in Great Britain 1985 by Colour Library Books Ltd.
CLB 1040
© 1985 Illustrations and text: Colour Library Books Ltd.,
    Guildford, Surrey, England.
Display and text filmsetting by Acesetters Ltd.,
    Richmond, Surrey, England.
Printed and bound in Barcelona, Spain by Rieusset and Eurobinder.
ISBN 0 86283 266 7
Dep.Leg. B-2863-85

2

As the campfire's pale and flickering light dances over the features of the gathered Maoris, an old man tells the tale of Maui, who went out in a canoe with his brothers and caught a massive fish...

After Maui brought it to the surface, his hungry brothers leapt from the canoe and began to eat the fish until only its backbone remained. Today, its skeleton lies exposed as the peaks, ridges and sweeping walls of rock that constitute the mountains of North Island. The canoe, riding gracefully over the sparkling waters of the Pacific Ocean and Tasman Sea, is South Island, crowned by the towering Southern Alps which lie wrapped in a year-round mantle of snow.

Rising high within the massifs, twenty peaks soar above 3,000 metres. Highest of all, Mount Cook stands at 3,762 metres, its precipitous faces swept by avalanches, its shoulders covered by roiling clouds – torn, rent and made ragged by the wind's irresistible force – and below, the jagged spikes of rock of the Southern Alps. The icy grip upon the mighty mountain ranges is sufficiently eased by the warm light of the sun to feed the streams with melted snow. Tumbling along burn and brook, the crystal waters race down to tarn and lake. Elsewhere, mighty falls stun the senses in plunging, roaring demonstrations of nature's savage might, and glaciers grind their way imperceptibly along the mountains' flanks.

Seiches that are seen on lakes are periodic rhythmical movements of the water caused by changes in atmospheric pressure or wind. At the lake called *Wakatipu* – 'space where the demon lies' – the Maoris know that it is caused by the beating heart of an evil giant. Who would doubt it in the solitude of evening when storm clouds blacken the sky, sonorous thunder rebounds from the lonesome hills and the very lake beneath one's gaze pulsates from the pumping of the sentient, malignant organ contained within the depths.

The geysers, mud pools and volcanoes of North Island are other fine examples of New Zealand's awesome, wild heritage. How could they have occurred, unless a *tohunga*, with magical powers, had been the cause? Lake Taupo is where such a man, Ngatoro-i-rangi, rested one day. When the clouds parted and Mt Tongariro stood revealed he decided to climb the awe-inspiring mountain, leaving his companions by the lake. He took his female slave, Auruhoe, with him and told his friends to fast while he was gone. Being hungry, they broke their word and the gods flung blizzards against the mountainside in their wrath. Ngatoro's prayers for the warmth of fire were whipped away by the winds and heard by the gods in Hawaiki. A stream of burning flame roared under the ground towards him, bursting through the surface in several places before it reached him, but too late to save his slave. However, in thanks for the help provided, he flung the woman's body into the newly-formed crater, known today as Ngauruhoe.

Land of legend, lake and mountain, New Zealand's untamed landscapes reflect the rugged individualism of its people; a young nation set amid dazzling displays from nature's unbound hand.

The Mount Hutt Range (above) contains one of the country's newest and most popular skiing resorts. Mount Cook National Park (facing page) stands high in the Southern Alps and offers some of the best mountain scenery in the world. Many of the rugged, snow-capped peaks rise to over 3,000 metres.

(Above) snowy peaks in the Stuart Mountains, South Island. The tumbling waters of the Poerua River (facing page) eventually flow into the Grey River. Bare stretches of shingle along the banks show the high level which the river can reach when swelled with melted snow after the spring thaw.

(Above) high ridges of the Southern Alps. The peaks and glaciers (facing page) of Mount Cook National Park. It was the race to conquer Mount Cook in the 1880s and '90s, more than anything else, that started New Zealand's interest in mountaineering.

(Above) the River Waiau flows from Lake Te Anau to Lake Manapouri, and thence to the sea at Te Waewae Bay. (Facing page) the spectacular cliffs of Milford Sound in Fiordland are part of a valley gouged from the rock by a glacier of the ice age.

The Waikato River (above), flows out of Lake Taupo near Nukuhau. (Facing page) Lake Wakatipu, where a combination of wind and water movements results in an unusual seiche which can raise the water level in one part of the lake while lowering it in another.

(Above) a tranquil Lake Taupo, with the snow-capped peaks of Tongariro National Park beyond.
The park was created in 1887, when the Tuwharetoa tribe gave these mountains to the nation,
including the symmetrical cone of Ngauruhoe (facing page), the country's most active volcanoe.

Beyond Ngauruhoe lies Ruapehu, which has a crater lake (above) only discovered in 1879 when George Beetham became the first man to climb the peak. (Facing page) Mount Ngauruhoe looms over the arid landscape south of Lake Taupo.

(Above) a beautiful highland stream flows swiftly over its bed of bare rocks. Lake Matheson (facing page) is a kettle lake, formed when blocks of subterranean ice, once buried beneath glaciers, melted, causing the collapse of the soil above, to form a depression.

Draining water from the Remarkables, by Lake Wakatipu (facing page), and from many hundreds of square kilometres of South Island, is the Clutha River (above). On its upper reaches, near the Old Man Range, is the important hydro-electric power station at Roxburgh.

The mighty Glacier in Mount Cook National Park (above), whose meltwaters flow into Lake Pukaki. Fox Glacier (facing page) is not only fed directly by snowfall on the névé, but also by the Albert, Jewel, Abel Jansen and Explorer glaciers high in the Southern Alps.

Previous page: (left) Lake Pukaki, fed by glacial meltwaters. (Right) rich pastureland near
Lake Hauroko, whose waters drain into Te Waewae Bay. The Tourist Hotel Corporation's Hermitage
(above) is virtually the only accommodation in the area around Mount Cook (facing page).

Otago Harbour (above) is a stretch of sheltered water which lies behind the Otago Peninsula, north of Dunedin. Overlooked by Ngauruhoe, Lake Taupo (facing page) covers almost 620 square kilometres, and is perfect for sailing and trout fishing.

Lake Tekapo (facing page) is one of several morainic lakes in the Mackenzie Country, west of Timaru.
The level of water in the lake is controlled by a cunningly concealed dam, which appears to be no
more than a road bridge. (Above) brooding clouds descend over the foothills of the Southern Alps.

The imposing conical mountain of Mitre Peak towers, shrouded in mist, above Milford Sound (facing page). (Above) the Mirror Lakes in their glacial valley, on the road from Milford to Te Anau.

The road to Milford Sound runs along the valley of the Eglinton River (above) for many kilometres, before climbing into the mountains beyond Lake Fergus towards the Homer Tunnel. (Facing page) rich pastures of the Canterbury Plains, in the east of South Island.

(Above) steep, dry slopes surround Lake Sarah. Near to Queenstown, on the shores of Lake Wakatipu in South Island, stand the jagged peaks of the mighty Remarkables (facing page).

(Facing page) a beautiful sunset over the unusual, Z-shaped Lake Wakatipu, which, although 84 km long, is only 5 km wide. Golden sunrise over the sea at Port Lyttelton, seen from Summit Road.

Lake Pearson (facing page) is justly famous for its trout fishing, the fish having been
introduced from Tasmania, to which they were introduced some years earlier from Britain.
Glendhu Bay (above) is one of the most tranquil spots on the shores of Lake Wanaka.

(Above) the wilderness lands around Lake Pukaki, and (facing page) the towering bulk of Mount Cook in the Southern Alps, seen reflected in the milky-blue waters of the lake.

There is rich pastureland along the banks of the Shotover River (above), which flows down from Lochnager into Lake Wakatipu, and in the Makarora Valley (facing page) sheep graze in the shadow of the towering Young Range.

The towering mass of Mount Egmont (these pages and overleaf) dominates New Plymouth (above). The rich soil of the region has been formed from the ash and rock thrown out from this volcanic mountain.